LOCOMOTIVES OF WESTERN CANADA

Mike Danneman

AMBERLEY

First published 2018

Amberley Publishing
The Hill, Stroud
Gloucestershire, GL5 4EP

www.amberley-books.com

Copyright © Mike Danneman, 2018

The right of Mike Danneman to be identified
as the Author of this work has been asserted in
accordance with the Copyrights, Designs and
Patents Act 1988.

ISBN 978 1 4456 8372 0 (print)
ISBN 978 1 4456 8373 7 (ebook)

British Library Cataloguing in Publication Data.
A catalogue record for this book is available from
the British Library.

Origination by Amberley Publishing.
Printed in the UK.

Introduction

As the country of Canada grew westward, so too did the railroads, and they were frequently intertwined with the budding country's politics. British Columbia joined the Canadian confederation in 1871 on the condition that a railroad would link the province to the rest of the county within ten years. The Canadian Pacific Railway (CPR) was incorporated on 21 October 1881 to build such a railroad to what is now Vancouver, and the promise was made good on 7 November 1885 with the completion of the line when the last spike was driven at Craigellachie, British Columbia. Southeastern British Columbia also saw CPR building a railway there to reach a fledgling silver strike, as well as countering a possible incursion of James J. Hill's Great Northern Railway from the United States. The Canadian Government provided grants for the construction of this secondary main line in exchange for permanent reduction of grain shipping rates (the Crow's Nest Pass Agreement of 1887), which would hinder the CPR for nearly 100 years in its ability to grow and improve its routes.

Meanwhile, Canadian Northern (CNoR) was begun in 1899 as a main line from Winnipeg to Vancouver through Edmonton, much of it well north of CPR's route. The route was finally completed to Vancouver in 1915, paralleling CPR through the rugged Thompson and Fraser River canyons, often building a railroad on a more torturous side of the river since CPR was there first. At the same time, Grand Trunk Pacific Railway (GTP) was incorporated in 1903 to build from Winnipeg to the Pacific, reaching the slow-developing seaport of Prince Rupert, and entering receivership in 1919. In the same timeframe CNoR ran out of money, and all government-owned railways, including CNoR, were brought under the name Canadian National Railways (CNR) on 20 December 1918. Not long after, in 1920, a failing GTP also became part of CNR.

Both CPR and CNR expanded further into the interiors of the western provinces with branch lines and eventually broadened their scope to become travel systems that included ships, hotels and even airlines. The Canadian Government maintained CNR as a Crown Corporation, gaining some critics, none louder than the successful CPR, who arguing that its taxes should not be used to fund a competitor. Early on, CNR was used as a method of the governmental colonising the underdeveloped regions of Western Canada, while CPR had the freedom to seek new business opportunities and link large population centers.

CPR and CNR utilised large rosters of steam locomotives to move all that newfound tonnage, many of which were built by the railroads' own shops and some specially designed to overcome steep mountain grades of Western Canada. In 1929, CPR received its first 2-10-4 locomotives, named after the Selkirk Mountains in which they served. They were the largest steam locomotives to operate in Canada and the British Empire. Like on most railroads in North America, the grip of steam locomotion was slow to release as diesel locomotive technology was still developing. Both CPR and CNR began to dieselise after the Second World War, finishing the conversion by 1960. The primal years saw both railroads having an eclectic roster of different diesels from early locomotive builders like Canadian Locomotive Works (CLC), Alco, Montreal Locomotive Works (MLW), Fairbanks Morse Co. and others.

In 1960, CNR became Canadian National, and in 1961 was 'rebranded' with a modern logo and colours, both of which are still in use today albeit slightly modified. CPR followed suit and modernised its image in 1968 with bright 'action red' colours and bold graphics, becoming CP Rail. Both railways have contributed much to what is considered standard in North American railroading today. CN introduced a wide-nose four-window 'comfort cab' on MLW M420 and Electro-Motive Division (EMD/ General Motors) GP38-2 models in 1973. These cabs were specially designed by the railroad, featuring increased collision protection and other crew amenities, while giving the face of diesel locomotives a new look, as well as being the predecessor to the safety cab. After a derailment in British Columbia, CN introduced ditch lights, which are lights mounted near the anti-climber on the front pilot of a locomotive. These lights help give better visibility around curves, with the added benefit of making trains more visible to the public at grade crossings. Moreover, both safety cabs and ditch lights have become standard on all North American freight locomotives.

Western Canada locomotive fleets today on CP and CN are composed of products by two builders – General Electric and EMD. CP Rail amassed a giant fleet of EMD/ General Motors diesel SD40-2 locomotives and became the third-largest owner of the model at 486 units, which ended up being backbone of the fleet for many years. In 1984, CP was the first railway in North America to develop AC traction for diesel-electric locomotives, and eventually became an owner of a huge group of AC locomotives from General Electric. CN's fleet has a bit more variety, with no one model making up the majority of the fleet.

Both railroads have acquired or merged smaller railroads into their fold. United States' Soo Line has physically disappeared into the CP and only exists as a name for reporting purposes in the US, while CN has swallowed Illinois Central in 1998 and several other smaller US railroads in recent years. CN also merged the British Columbia Railway (BC Rail) into its fold in 2004. All of these 'fallen flags' have added a little variety to the CP and CN paint schemes in recent years, and today CP operates a 12,400-mile system while CN runs an impressive 20,421-mile railway.

What follows is a photographic look at the locomotives of Western Canada since the year 2000. First, we'll look the locomotives in scenic locations on the CP line from Calgary to Kamloops, and then CN's line west of Edmonton to Kamloops. Then we'll follow CP on the southern Crowsnest Pass route west and up the scenic Windermere Subdivision. The last group of images will illustrate both CP and CN as they snake through rugged canyons to Vancouver. Enjoy the journey!

A Canadian Pacific intermodal train thunders by a westbound passenger special at Bearspaw, Alberta, on 1 October 2010. The eastbound train is led by single CP General Electric AC4400CW No. 9615, with two more high-horsepower GE DPU (Distributed Power Unit) locomotives entrained in the long intermodal. Bearspaw Siding is 14 miles west of Calgary on the CP's Laggan Subdivision.

A short two-car Canadian Pacific local is westbound as it passes the emerald waters of the Bow River just out of Exshaw, Alberta, on 24 September 2013. Four-axle locomotives Nos 3054 and 3102 are GMD GP38AC models built in London, Ontario, in 1986.

Canadian Pacific GE AC4400CWs Nos 9626 and 9664 power an empty eastbound Canpotex potash train into the west end of the siding at Banff, Alberta, on the morning of 20 September 2002. Both locomotives are part of a 101-unit order of AC4400CWs that CP purchased from GE, delivered between September 1997 and January 1998.

On the morning of 20 September 2002, a westbound Canadian Pacific intermodal train flies along the Bow River in scenic Banff National Park at Castle Mountain, Alberta. A pair of GE AC4400CWs power the westbound, led by No. 8653, which was delivered new to the railroad in November 2001.

A light dusting of some of the season's first snow decorates the high peaks in the background as an eastbound Canadian Pacific freight arcs along the Bow River at Castle Mountain, Alberta, on 20 September 2002. Three GE AC4400CW locomotives are up front, with the two red CP units bracketing a leased blue CEFX No. 1017.

An eastbound Canadian Pacific grain train led by GE ES44AC No. 8856 and three more GE locomotives sweeps through Morant's Curve east of Lake Louise, Alberta, on 13 July 2013. The curve is named for long-time CP company photographer Nicholas Morant, who spent nearly his entire fifty-year career with CP and made the location famous with his photography.

Led by GE ES44AC No. 8744, an eastbound Canadian Pacific intermodal train cants around the famous Morant's Curve east of Lake Louise, Alberta, on 27 June 2006. This location is in Banff National Park and is easily accessed via the Bow River Parkway.

Canadian Pacific's Royal Canadian Pacific luxury train pauses at Lake Louise, Alberta, on 13 September 2002. The classy train is pulled by an A-B-A set of GMD F units led by FP7 No. 1400, F9B No. 1900 and a former Canadian National/VIA Rail FP9 now numbered 1401. During the station stop, a westbound sulphur train rumbles by on the new north track climbing the pass.

Cresting the summit of Kicking Horse Pass at Divide, Alberta, is the westbound Royal Canadian Pacific passenger train on 20 September 2002, pulled by GMD FP7 No. 1400, FP9 No. 1401 and GP38-2 No. 3084. GMD freight locomotive No. 3084, built in 1986, was originally painted in CP Rail 'action orange' colours, but was repainted tuscan and grey in March 2000 to help out with passenger duties when needed.

A westbound Canadian Pacific intermodal train led by EMD SD9043MAC No. 9134 at Yoho, British Columbia, drops downgrade between the Spiral Tunnels at Kicking Horse Pass on 20 September 2002. Massive No. 9134 is one of sixty-one SD9043MACs (Nos 9100–9160) owned by the railroad, most of which were assembled by CP in its own Ogden Shops in Calgary. Only Nos 9100–9111 were built by GMD in London, Ontario.

Even beautiful in the rain, a westbound Canadian Pacific train led by lone GE AC4400CW No. 8742 drops into Field, British Columbia, amid the Canadian Rockies, on 18 July 2011. The weather changes quickly up here though; by the time the mid-train DPU, No. 8563, rolled by, it was in full sun.

Canadian Pacific's Royal Canadian Pacific luxury train drops off the steep grade over Kicking Horse Pass at Field, British Columbia, on a gorgeous 13 September 2002. The train will stop for a brief crew change at Field before continuing on to Golden. GMD FP7 No. 1400 was originally built as CP No. 4099 in April 1953 and was unfortunately retired in December 2011.

Time to go to work in Field, as a CP crew member heads to his train on 16 September 2002. CP acquired a huge fleet of EMD/GMD SD40-2s numbering 486 units, with one of these machines, No. 6027, being built in December 1982. By this time a couple of decades later, a number of the locomotives were converted to B unit status and were to be operated as a trailing locomotive only, with plated windows being an obvious sign of such service, as on No. 5771.

Canadian Pacific EMD SD9043MAC No. 9141 basks in a fleeting moment of afternoon sun at Field, British Columbia, on 16 September 2002. CP rostered sixty-one of these 4,300 hp locomotives, built in 1998–99, and they were meant to be eventually converted to 6,000 hp engines, hence the '43' in the model designation. However, none of these conversions were ever done and the locomotives fell out of favour, with most of them going into storage whenever CP traffic levels dropped.

Passing a reflective mountain lake, a westbound Canadian Pacific grain train departs Field, British Columbia, on 23 September 2013. Powering the train is GE ES44AC No. 8756, with No. 9379 in the lead and GE AC4400CW No. 9727 as the rear DPU locomotive.

A Canadian Pacific grain train heads west under stormy weather during a brief instant of sunshine at Ottertail, British Columbia, on 23 September 2013. CP has 291 of these ES44AC locomotives on the roster, which were built by General Electric between 2005 and 2012.

Grand mountain scenery abounds on 13 September 2002 as Canadian Pacific's westbound Royal Canadian Pacific luxury train meets the Rocky Mountaineer Railtours passenger train at Leanchoil, British Columbia, amid the splendour of the Canadian Rockies. Leanchoil is a 9,468-foot siding 16.9 miles from Field on CP's Mountain Subdivision.

Curving along the Kicking Horse River, a bright Canadian Pacific stack train lights up a dreary day as it approaches Glenogle, British Columbia, on 22 September 2013. CP GE ES44AC No. 8847 leads two older GE AC4400CWs as power for the westbound train.

Canadian Pacific train 177 west is pulled by three matching Multi-mark CP Rail SD40-2s as the train approaches Glenogle, British Columbia, on 16 September 2002. This location is dramatically different now, as Trans-Canada 1 is now located high above this site, where the faint earth-colored line is on the tree-covered mountain on the right. The old highway bridge over the railroad and Kicking Horse River is now gone too.

A Rocky Mountaineer Railtours passenger train curves eastbound out of Glenogle, British Columbia, on 16 September 2002. Powering the train are a pair of former Canadian National safety cab-equipped GMDs, GP40-2Ws Nos 8014 and 8012. These excursion trains operate over both CN and CP, running on CP between Kamloops and Calgary.

A westbound Canadian Pacific vehicle train passes another westbound freight at Moberly, just west of Golden, British Columbia, on 12 July 2013. GE ES44AC No. 8781 was built in late 2006 and is leading the train up toward a mountain crossing of Rogers Pass inside the Mount Macdonald Tunnel.

A westbound Canadian Pacific intermodal train passes a set of helpers at Rogers, British Columbia, on 16 September 2002. Some maintenance work was being done on the Mount Macdonald Tunnel, requiring some westbound trains to use the older, steeper main line through the Connaught Tunnel, and briefly requiring the use of helpers out of Rogers once again.

A westbound Canadian Pacific coal train emerges from the Mount Macdonald Tunnel powered by ES44AC No. 8891 on Rogers Pass, British Columbia, on 23 July 2011. According to the Canadian Railway Hall of Fame, it is the longest railroad tunnel in the Western Hemisphere at 14.6 kilometres, or just over 9 miles (9.1). The tunnel allows westbound CP trains to cross the formidable Rogers Pass – a lower-elevation crossing of the Selkirk Mountains.

On an arresting 25 September 2012 afternoon, a Canadian Pacific coal train emerges from the Mount Macdonald Tunnel in the enchanting mountains of British Columbia. The sensation of listening to a train climbing through the tunnel for over twenty minutes is an acoustic treat, and with CP providing an almost new GE ES44AC No. 9353 to pull the train, the shiny red beacon among the incredible Canadian Rockies becomes a sensuous delight.

A Canadian Pacific freight heads westbound west of Ross Peak, British Columbia, on 23 July 2011. This location is on CP's scenic Rogers Pass through the Selkirk Mountains, not far from the western portal of Mount Macdonald Tunnel. CP Nos 8777 and 8753 are both GE ES44ACs and were delivered in 2006 and 2005 respectively.

Departing Begbie on the west side of Revelstoke, British Columbia, is a westbound Canadian Pacific ballast extra on the pretty autumn afternoon of 29 September 2015. The ten-car train is powered by CP No. 5003, a SD30C-ECO rebuilt from EMD SD40-2 No. 5983 and now sporting a longer 'snoot-style' nose and flared radiators to support the cooling system required for the lower emission engine now equipped inside the locomotive.

On the morning of 30 September 2015, an eastbound Canadian Pacific coal empty passes Begbie as it arrives at Revelstoke, British Columbia, for a crew change. Two of CP's GE ES44ACs are on the head end of the train, with another being used as a lone DPU locomotive on the rear of the coal empty headed back to the Alberta coalfields near Sparwood for reloading.

An eastbound Rocky Mountaineer Railtours passenger train crosses the Columbia River, entering Revelstoke, British Columbia, on the early autumn day of 30 September 2015. The unique paint scheme on the train was applied in 2011–12 and the train is led by former Canadian National safety cab-equipped GMD GP40-2W No. 8012.

Eastbound Canadian Pacific coal train 840 crosses the Columbia River, entering Revelstoke, British Columbia, on the delightful autumn day of 29 September 2015. Built around 1970, this is the third CP railroad bridge spanning the river here.

Canadian Pacific intermodal train 199 rolls across the Columbia River at Revelstoke, British Columbia, on 30 September 2015. On 4 May 2013, much of the wooden deck of this bridge burned in a smoky and spectacular blaze, but the damage to the bridge itself was minimal, with CP quickly repairing and opening it back up to traffic by 5 May.

Westbound Canadian Pacific potash train 675 snakes along the Eagle River at East Taft, British Columbia, on 23 July 2011. Two of the railroad's omnipresent GE AC4400CWs power the train through the lush scenery on this part of the CP's Shuswap Subdivision main line, west of Revelstoke.

As a rancher cuts hay inside the Canadian Pacific's horseshoe curve between Carlin and Notch Hill, British Columbia, a westbound freight climbs the grade through the big curve on 23 July 2011. General Electric AC4400CW No. 8635, built in 2001, leads the train consisting of mostly grain loads.

A Canadian National freight rumbles over the Pembina River Bridge between Entwistle and Evansburg, Alberta, on CN's Edson Subdivision toward the end of the day on 4 August 2016. Powering the train are two CN EMD SD75Is, Nos 5686 and 5709, both of which were built in 1996. This train is travelling westbound on the CN's Edson Subdivision out of the Edmonton area.

Connecting with the Edson Subdivision at Bickerdike, Alberta, CN's Foothills Subdivision heads south (timetable west) destined for several coal mines and a rock quarry. A westbound Canadian National coal train bound for loading at Coal Valley pops out of the 591-foot tunnel at mile 33.4 just west (south) of Robb, Alberta, on 8 August 2016.

Canadian National coal train 769 travels up the Luscar Industrial Spur near Cadomin, Alberta, on 15 July 2013. The strange jog in the track about twelve cars back is where a switch was once located for a track operating to the Gregg River loadout, which was torn out around 2010.

A Canadian National empty coal train heads up the Luscar Industrial Spur near Cadomin, Alberta, on 8 August 2016. This is the third section of a 150-car train – steep 3 per cent grades on this spur out of Leyland make this necessary. Much of the past mining activity has now been reclaimed in the area, with the green grasses now covering the rolling hillsides attracting a lot of grazing wildlife and, in turn, grizzly bears…

Canadian National coal train 769 loads at Teck's Luscar Mine near Cadomin, Alberta, on 15 July 2013. Afternoon sunlight turns the Luscar Mine coal processing plant into interesting geometric shapes as the train slowly loads on the spur. This loadout is part of Teck's Cardinal River Operation and is located on a line operating out of Leyland called the Luscar Industrial Spur, which is located at the highest elevation on the Canadian National system.

At Teck's Cardinal River Operation near Cadomin, Alberta, on 8 August 2016, a third section of a Canadian National coal train prepares to load its fifty cars and is running through the loader so the operator can make an inspection of the empty cars before loading can commence. The train will load with two GE ES44ACs on the head end, but once finished CN No. 2958 will be left on the rear of the train and No. 2900 moved to the other end to be used as lead power. This train will combine with the other two sections currently waiting at Bickerdike (near Edson), and will then move west for export.

Eastbound Canadian National train 412 passes through Hargwen, Alberta, on the morning of 20 July 2011. Leading the train is a recently repainted General Electric C40-8M No. 2400. CN has fifty-five of these specially design cowl locomotives, which were built in 1990 and 1992. With the BC Rail acquisition in July 2004, the railroad picked up twenty-six more copies of this unique engine, upgraded by BCR to 4,400 horsepower and Dash 9 specifications and labelled C40-8Mu.

After years spent hustling intermodal across the south-western deserts of the United States, some of Santa Fe's Super Fleet have been exiled to a similar, yet completely different duty hauling trains across the northernmost transcontinental in North America. From cactus to pine trees, two Canadian National GE C40-8Ws Nos 2138 and 2158 (former Santa Fe/BNSF Nos 806 and 846 in Warbonnet days) rumble eastward with double-stacked intermodal train 116 at Pedley, Alberta, on 16 July 2013.

Canadian National train 412 crosses Prairie Creek Bridge as it approaches Hinton, Alberta, on the morning of 16 July 2013. This eastbound freight train is powered by a pair of General Electric locomotives – ES44DC No. 2220 and C40-8M cowl No. 2415.

With the sunshine about to disappear under some early day clouds, Canadian National train 104 traverses Prairie Creek Bridge at Hinton, Alberta, heading east on CN's Edson Subdivision on 19 July 2013.

A pair of Canadian National EMD SD70M-2s powers westbound CN train 111 east of Entrance, Alberta, on the afternoon of 13 July 2013. The small community of Entrance received its name from being the first CNR station east of the entrance to Jasper Park, which today is the world-famous Jasper National Park.

Canadian National train 106 crosses the Athabasca River Bridge just east of Solomon, Alberta, on 13 July 2013. Powering the eastbound intermodal train are GE C44-9W No. 2706 and ES44DC No. 2333. CN was a late converter to AC traction locomotives, finally buying GE ES44ACs in late 2012.

With a noisy thunderstorm brewing to the east, Canadian National manifest freight 417 sails over the Athabasca River east of Solomon, Alberta, on 9 July 2014. CN No. 2597 is a GE C44-9W, and trailing is older sister GE C40-8M cowl locomotive No. 2452.

Canadian National EMD SD70M-2 No. 8883 leads a Sultrans unit sulphur train westbound along the Athabasca River at Solomon, Alberta, on the afternoon of 9 July 2014. CN has 190 4,300 horsepower SD70M-2 units built by EMD between 2005 and 2010, numbered 8000–8024 and 8800–8964.

An eastbound Canadian National freight curves through Solomon, Alberta, on CN's Edson Subdivision on the morning of 7 August 2016. CN No. 3015, a GE ET44AC, was built in the summer of 2015. These locomotives are Tier 4 compliant, meaning they satisfy more stringent emission standards for locomotives built in 2015 or later. The larger, more angular rear radiator section, along with a boxy hood section around the exhaust stack, is indicative of these standards being met, with added cooling capacity along with further exhaust treatments.

On the lovely afternoon of 7 July 2014, Canadian National train 310 arcs through Robertson's Curve as it departs Swan Landing, Alberta, along Brûlé Lake. CN EMD SD75I No. 5756 leads a pair of GE C44-9Ws, Nos 2577 and 2599, and EMD SD70M-2 No. 8883 through this scenic setting just east of Jasper National Park.

It's getting close to sunset at 8:55 p.m. on 19 July 2013 at Swan Landing, Alberta, as Canadian National westbound train 193 passes the shores of a tranquil Brûlé Lake. Pastel shades begin to colour the brighter parts of the scene just east of Jasper National Park, signalling the end of another day.

The spectacular Brûlé Range nicely reflects on the calm surface of Brûlé Lake as VIA Rail's eastbound *Canadian* rolls through Robertson's Curve at Swan Landing, Alberta, on the afternoon of 7 July 2014. VIA EMD F40PH-3 Nos 6407, 6443 and 6408 power the twenty-one-car passenger train, which is almost exclusively made up of Budd-built stainless steel cars built for Canadian Pacific in 1954–55.

Canadian National train 416 curves out of Swan Landing, Alberta, on 7 July 2014. This train is powered by GE ES44DC No. 2335 and EMD SD75I No. 5680 and is passing through this scenic location just east of Brûlé, near the eastern border of Jasper National Park.

On the afternoon of 12 July 2014, GE C40-8M cowl locomotive No. 2403 leads Canadian National train 347 through Brûlé Tunnel toward Park Gate, Alberta, entering Jasper National Park. Brûlé Tunnel is a 735-foot bore from mile 204.8 to 205.1 on CN's Edson Subdivision.

Canadian National train 180 curves into Brûlé Tunnel, just east of Park Gate, Alberta, on 12 July 2014. The train is about to exit Jasper National Park, with the actual border directly on top of the tunnel. Trailing GE C44-9W No. 2551 is black Illinois Central EMD SD70 No. 1030, which joined the CN roster with the acquisition of IC in July 1999.

On the eastern boundary of Jasper National Park, Canadian National train 303 is passing through Brûlé Tunnel approaching Park Gate, Alberta, on the afternoon of 12 July 2014. Leading the train is CN EMD SD70ACe No. 8101, still in blue and grey EMD demonstrator paint. So far, CN has only purchased four AC traction locomotives from builder EMD, all of which are former demonstrator units.

On 19 July 2011, Canadian National intermodal train 111 heads west at Windy Point, near Snaring, Alberta, along Jasper Lake in scenic Jasper National Park. Powering the kaleidoscopic train of double-stacked containers is an equally colourful locomotive consist of CN GE ES44DC No. 2299, BC Rail GE C40-8Mu No. 4617 and CN EMD No. 8956.

Canadian National train 304 approaches Windy Point, west of Devona, Alberta, in alluring Jasper National Park on the afternoon of 10 July 2014. The varied locomotive set consists of CN GE C40-8W No. 2151, Illinois Central EMD SD70 No. 1033, EMD SD70M-2 No. 8884 and GE C44-9W No. 2641. Lead unit CN No. 2151 is former Santa Fe Warbonnet-painted No. 832, which was bought used from BNSF.

Along beautiful Jasper Lake and the rugged scenery in Jasper National Park, Canadian National train 117 passes Windy Point, west of Devona, Alberta, on 16 July 2013. This westbound train only has a few more miles before a quick crew change at Jasper. Locomotives for the train are CN EMD SD70M-2 No. 8884 and solid dark blue BC Rail GE C44-9W No. 4651.

On the morning of 19 July 2011, a Canadian National grain train heads west through Henry House, Alberta. This location was named after William Henry of the North West Co., who built a trading post at the junction of the Miette and Athabasca rivers near present-day Jasper.

While Jasper is under dark, stormy skies, eastbound Canadian National sulphur train 712 crosses the Snaring River at Henry House, Alberta, on 19 July 2011. Lone CN GE ES44DC No. 2238 powers the train eastbound over the Edson Subdivision toward Edmonton. CN rosters 125 of these ES44DC models, which were built by GE between January 2006 and October 2010.

The engineer of Canadian National train 112 visually inspects the passing cars of westbound CN train 417 at Henry House, Alberta, on 17 July 2013. Even though GE ES44AC No. 2813 was built only months earlier, it is already showing signs of heavy use on the CN main line.

Canadian National train 302 passes along the shore of a pristine lake at Henry House, Alberta, amid the splendour of Jasper National Park on a stunning 8 July 2014. GE C44-9W No. 2201 and EMD SD75I No. 5718 provide motive power for the eastbound train.

Canadian National local train 513 passes a mountain lake at Henry House, Alberta, at 8:29 p.m. on 11 July 2014. The Hinton to Jasper (and return) local is powered by a vintage pair of aging GMDs – SD40-2W No. 5246 and SD40u No. 6011 – which are battle-worn, but still able to haul plenty of tonnage on CN's main line, just as General Motors Diesel Division envisioned.

Outpacing thunderstorms moving in quickly from the north-east, VIA Rail's westbound *Canadian* passes a pristine mountain lake at Henry House, Alberta, on 9 August 2016. The train will finally get a drenching from the weather at the station and service stop of Jasper.

EMD SD60F cowl No. 5518 leads a second section of Canadian National train 847 through Jasper National Park at Henry House, Alberta, on 11 July 2014. GMD SD50F and SD60F locomotives have cowled rear hoods that are equipped with the innovative 'Draper Taper' – the so-called tapered notch cut into the car body just behind the cab so the train crew has some sight line backwards. This feature was the creation of CN Assistant Chief of Motive Power William L. Draper.

Curving through English, Alberta, on a sunny 5 August 2016 is a westbound Canadian National intermodal train. Leading the train is lone GE ET44AC No. 3045, which was built in 2016 and is still arrestingly clean. The train will soon be arriving at Jasper Yard for a quick crew change.

A westbound Canadian National unit train, with sulphur cars up front and grain hoppers on the rear, passes through English, Alberta, on 5 August 2016. CN No. 2800 – a General Electric ES44AC, which was built in September 2012 – is the railroad's first AC traction locomotive.

Canadian National's main line through Jasper can be very busy at times. Here, eastbound Canadian National train 302 meets westbound CN train 111 on the curves through English, Alberta, on a rainy 14 July 2013. Both trains are led by GE ES44DC locomotives.

Canadian National had sixty cowl-body SD50Fs built by GMD in 1985 and 1987. In this view on 19 September 2002 at English, Alberta, a CN intermodal train approaches Jasper with GMD SD50F No. 5418 leading the westbound train. These unique locomotives were all retired from the roster in late 2008. Five ended up in the US on two short lines, with Nos 5402, 5411 and 5416 going to the Dakota, Missouri Valley & Western Railroad, and Nos 5404 and 5438 serving Montana Limestone Co. in Warren, Montana. Unfortunately, the rest have been cut up for scrap.

VIA Rail's eastbound train 2, the *Canadian*, leaves Jasper at English, Alberta, over the Canadian National Edson Subdivision main line on 18 September 2002. Two GMD F40PH-2 locomotives pull the twenty-one-car train, with No. 6441 leading the way.

Canadian National train 348 climbs out of Jasper, Alberta, at English on 14 July 2013. Powering the eastbound train are GE ES44DC No. 2233 and BC Rail C40-8Mu No. 4608. From this angle, it is possible to see the Draper Taper notch cut into the cowl car body just behind the cab, seen on CN SD50Fs and SD60F GMDs, along with the C40-8M/C40-8Mu units from GE.

Brand-new Canadian National GE C44-9Ws Nos 2644 and 2647 power an eastbound coal train that has just departed Jasper at English, Alberta, on 19 September 2002. This series of GE C44-9W locomotives, Nos 2200–2205 and Nos 2523–2727, along with early ES44DCs Nos 2220–2289, all have the unique 'tear drop' windshields unique to CN.

Under a stormy sky in Jasper, Alberta, on 17 September 2002, GMD SD40-2 No. 5320 is leading a westbound train through the yard. This 1979, GMD-built locomotive features the CN-designed comfort cab that provides better collision protection, as well as crew comforts such as refrigerators, hot plates and coffeepots. This cab design became a CN signature for a decade and a half, and became the inspiration for all safety-cab locomotives built henceforth for service in North America.

VIA Rail's train 5, the *Skeena*, on the left, passes train 2, the *Canadian*, on the station track at Jasper, Alberta, on 18 September 2002. The *Skeena* is heading for the wye to turn the entire consist so it is ready to depart westbound later that afternoon. Both *Skeena*'s and *Canadian*'s schedules connected at Jasper for ease of transferring trains. Both are powered by GMD F40PH-2 locomotives specially designed for passenger service, being equipped with a 500 kW generator off the prime mover to power the passenger consist for lights, heating and cooling.

VIA Rail's train 1, the *Canadian*, pulls into Jasper, Alberta, on 16 July 2013. In a few moments, passengers can stretch their legs in this scenic mountain town while an armada of workers clean and prepare the train for the trip west. On the left is unassigned VIA F40PH-3 No. 6412, which is being used as a protection locomotive for trains 1 and 2, and 5 and 6. These locomotives are former GMD F40PH-2s that have been rebuilt between 2009 and 2012 with a standalone HEP generator, as well as other improvements, and are labelled F40PH-3s.

VIA Rail GMD F40PH-2 sits at Jasper, Alberta, on 17 September 2002. This is the original paint scheme for these locomotives, which were built between 1986 and 1989 in London, Ontario. Fifty-four units will later be rebuilt into F40PH-3s, extending their service life by another fifteen to twenty years.

A couple of thunderstorms continue to build east of Jasper, Alberta, on the afternoon of 7 August 2016. Just west of the station, VIA Rail GMD F40PH-3 No. 6455 rests on a spur track and is being used as protection power for trains 1 and 2, and 5 and 6. Canadian National's main line through town is busy too as CN No. 102 arrives for a crew change, while in the background a westbound is about ready to head out.

On a stormy afternoon in Jasper, Alberta, a westbound Canadian National freight departs Jasper Yard into a moment of sunshine on 18 September 2002. CN No. 5367, an EMD SD40-2, was built for Missouri Pacific in 1973 and was acquired from Union Pacific in 1994.

BC Rail (formerly British Columbia Railway) GE C44-9WL No. 4644 leads Canadian National train 102 at control point Home entering Jasper, Alberta, on the beautiful morning of 5 August 2016. BCR No. 4644 is one of four built for the railroad in 1995 and painted in British Columbia's Provincial colours of red, white and blue. Ten more C44-9Ws later built for BC Rail were delivered in a solid dark blue scheme.

Passing milepost 8 on Canadian National's Albreda Subdivision while running west out of Jasper is CN train 196, working through Geikie, Alberta, on 11 July 2014. Lone CN EMD SD70M-2 No. 8805 powers the big double-stack intermodal train eastbound.

It's a beautiful day at Jasper, Alberta, on 20 July 2013, as Canadian National intermodal train 117 approaches milepost 8 just east of Geikie on CN's Albreda Subdivision. The train is about to cross a pedestrian grade crossing for a national park trail to Virl, Dorothy and Christine lakes.

Canadian National train 348 hustles empty coal gons past mile 10.3 west of Geikie, Alberta, on 7 July 2014. Leading the train is CN No. 5606, one of twenty-six EMD SD70I locomotives built for the railroad in 1995. These SD70Is are 4,000 hp, while newer SD75Is are 4,300 hp, with the 'I' in both model designations representing an isolated cab, also called a 'WhisperCab'.

VIA Rails's *Canadian* cruises over the top of Yellowhead Pass, British Columbia, on 20 July 2011. Leading loco F40PH-3 No. 6457 has recently been rebuilt and is decked out in VIA's current locomotive paint scheme of green, silver and gold (yellow), while trailing F40PH-2 No. 6451 is still in older paint. Soon the train will make the lengthy station stop at Jasper, letting people enjoy some fresh air amid the ravishing Canadian Rockies.

A Canadian National freight passes through Geikie, Alberta, on 18 September 2002. The locomotives leading the train west on the Albreda Subdivision on this wet autumn day are EMD SD75I No. 5655 and GMD SD50F No. 5449.

Climbing Yellowhead Pass from the west, an eastbound Canadian National freight thunders past the signals at mile 22.9 between Fitzwilliam and Yellowhead, British Columbia, on 5 August 2016. CN's first two groups of EMD SD70M-2s, Nos 8000–8019 and Nos 8020–8024, built in late 2005 and early 2006, all have high headlights mounted above the cab windows.

Canadian National train 304 rumbles eastbound along the shore of Moose Lake, British Columbia, at milepost 40 on CN's Albreda Subdivision on 14 July 2014. The mountainside above the train is covered with dead trees, which had recently been attacked by a widespread pine beetle infestation.

A manifest freight from Prince Rupert, Canadian National train 323 heads west at Von Zuben, British Columbia, on 14 July 2014. This location got its interesting name from Raphael Leonard von Zuben, a Canadian National purchasing agent, who assisted the railroad with exploring the Canadian Rockies.

Canadian National train 117 passes through Wolfenden, British Columbia, on CN's Clearwater Subdivision on 21 July 2011. The westbound train is powered by GE ES44DC No. 2340, built a year before, in 2010, and older GE sister C44-9W No. 2562, built in December 1997.

On 21 July 2011, Canadian National train 117 passes through Louis Creek, British Columbia. Although the mountainsides are now greening up, damage from a major forest fire that swept through the area in 2003 can still be seen. Louis Creek was the site of a major sawmill that burned in the devastating fire and was never rebuilt.

Canadian Pacific's Royal Canadian Pacific luxury train crosses the massive bridge at Lethbridge, Alberta, on CP's Crowsnest Pass route on 15 September 2002. The huge structure, commonly known as Lethbridge Viaduct or High Level Bridge, was built by CP between 1907 and 1909 to replace a smaller, older wooden bridge located on a more circuitous and steep former route across the valley. The bridge is 1,624 meters (5,328 feet) long (yes, over a mile long!) and is 96 meters (314 feet) above Oldman River. It is the largest railway structure in Canada and the largest bridge of its type in the world.

On the clear morning of 22 September 2002, the Royal Canadian Pacific luxury train leaves the mountains behind as it swings through a gentle curve at milepost 44 between Chokio and Piegan, Alberta, on the CP's line over Crowsnest Pass.

An eastbound Canadian Pacific freight heads into the morning sun, leaving Lundbreck, Alberta, on 28 September 2010. The train is powered by Union Pacific EMD SD9043MAC No. 8301 and CP GE ES44AC No. 8778. UP power is common on the Cranbrook and Crowsnest Subdivisions, and during this era UP SD9043MACs were very prevalent on the line.

Glowing in a rising sun, Canadian Pacific's Royal Canadian Pacific luxury passenger train leaves Crowsnest Pass as the moon sets over the mountains east of Lundbreck, Alberta, at the crack of dawn on 22 September 2002. Powering the train are GMD FP7 No. 1400, GMD FP9 No. 1401 and GMD GP38-2 No. 3084.

An eastbound Canadian Pacific freight is passing through the former town of Frank, Alberta, on CP's Crowsnest Pass line on 28 September 2010. At 4:10 a.m. on 29 April 1903, 82 million tons of rock fell from the summit of Turtle Mountain into the Crowsnest River valley below, covering a portion of the CP and nearly wiping out the town of Frank. At least ninety people were killed in the ninety seconds in which the slide occurred. The original site of the town was later abandoned because of the unstable nature of the mountain above. In this view, the train is passing some of the debris from the massive slide, as rain storms brew over Crowsnest Pass in the background.

Passing through scenic Crowsnest Pass at Sentinel, Alberta, on 10 October 2017 is an eastbound Canadian Pacific freight. Splicing CP ES44AC Nos 8797 and 8786 is Warbonnet-clad BNSF GE C44-9W No. 785, looking a bit out of place. It is unusual to see a BNSF unit working over Crowsnest.

A special train for the Children's Wish Foundation of Canada operated over portions of the Canadian Pacific's system in the summer of 2011. Here, CP GP38-2 No. 3084 leads the special up Crowsnest Pass, British Columbia, headed into McGillivray Loop at a location now called Fabro on 17 July 2011.

A westbound Canadian Pacific grain train led by two Union Pacific EMD SD9043MACs approaches historic Crowsnest Pass, Alberta, on 28 September 2010, and will soon be crossing into British Columbia. With the locomotive pool agreement between CP and UP between Calgary and Spokane, pure sets of UP power on this line are commonplace.

Heading for Crowsnest Pass, CP's Royal Canadian Pacific luxury tour train meets a westbound CP freight utilising Natal Siding near Sparwood, British Columbia, on the afternoon of 14 September 2002. A beaver was first part of the CPR logo in 1886, and the logo on the nose of No. 1400 was used from 1949 to 1959, while GE AC4400CW No. 8607 carries a modern version of it, used from 1997 to 2007.

A westbound Canadian Pacific freight curves through Elko, British Columbia, led by Union Pacific No. 8307 on 17 July 2011. UP No. 8307 is a 4,300 hp EMD SD9043MAC that was built in 1999 and was eventually meant to be converted to a 6,000 hp engine, hence the '43' in the model designation. However, none of these conversions were ever done, and UP ended up with the largest group of the model at 309 units of the 410 built.

Canadian Pacific GE AC4400CW No. 9584 leads an eastbound empty coal gons into Elko, British Columbia, on 14 September 2002. CP No. 9584 was built by GE in September 1997, and is one of 438 AC4400CWs bought by the railroad between 1995 and 2004.

After the passengers toured Fort Steele, CP's Royal Canadian Pacific luxury train headed east toward Crowsnest Pass at Wardner, British Columbia, on 14 September 2002. The classy train of mostly heavyweight business cars is powered by an A-B-A set of GMD-built F units led by FP7 No. 1400, F9B No. 1900 and a former Canadian National/VIA Rail FP9 now numbered 1401.

On 11 October 2017, autumn colour abounds along the Kootenay River as an eastbound Canadian Pacific coal empty leaves Fort Steele, British Columbia. The train is headed for loading on the Fording River Subdivision, a 32.6-mile coal branch out of Sparwood, Alberta.

Just after changing crews on the wye at Fort Steele, British Columbia, a Canadian Pacific unit potash train curves on the main line toward Crowsnest Pass on the morning of 11 October 2017. A pair of Union Pacific GE ES44ACs bracket CP and CEFX AC4400CWs as power for the eastbound train. In the background, the wayfreight and another potash train sit in the small yard at Fort Steele, with the local waiting to go north on the Windermere Subdivision to Golden.

A pair of Canadian Pacific GMD SD40-2s switches the small yard at Cranbrook, British Columbia, at the end of a rainy 14 July 2011. The historic covered water tank still survives (although moved from its original location) as part of the Cranbrook Railroad Museum.

While GMD GP38-2 Nos 3041 and 3029 switch Cranbrook yard on 14 September 2002, the switchman looking over his list as he takes a short rest beneath the light pole. On the main line next to the switch job is an eastbound Canpotex potash unit train led by leased CEFX EMD SD9043MAC No. 113. For many years CP has had long-term leases of these 4,300 hp EMD locomotives, as well as GE AC4400CWs, from CIT Group/Capital Finance.

Canadian Pacific EMD SD40-2F No. 9005 sits in front of the yard office at Cranbrook, British Columbia, on the afternoon of 27 June 2006. More than two years after EMD built its last SD40-2 model, CP Rail took delivery of twenty-five custom units built at GMD in London, Ontario, in November 1988. These have the Draper Taper cut out in the cowl body, like CN's SD50F/60Fs, and their bright paint scheme slathered over a large cowled body later earned them the affectionate nickname 'Red Barns'.

A double rainbow encircles a pair of venerable Canadian Pacific EMD SD40-2s after a good rainstorm in Cranbrook, British Columbia, on 4 October 2010. CP No. 5915 was built in October 1979, while younger sister No. 6031, trailing behind, was outshopped in January 1983.

A Canadian Pacific manifest freight follows the shore of Moyie Lake just east of Moyie, British Columbia, on 21 July 2013. General Electric ES44AC No. 8921 leads three AC4400CW locomotives for power on this eastbound train on CP's Moyie Subdivision, which runs from Cranbrook to the international boundary at Kingsgate.

A Canadian Pacific freight from Cranbrook to Nelson curves along the shore of Moyie Lake near Moyie, British Columbia. Three CP Rail EMD SD40-2s lead the westbound train near sunset on the delightful early summer day of 27 June 2006.

Blue CEFX GE AC4400CW No. 1046 leads a westbound Canadian Pacific freight along the shore of Moyie Lake at Moyie, British Columbia, on 28 June 2006. CP has long-term leases on quite a few locomotives from CEFX. In fact, No. 1046 is still running on CP today!

A westbound Canadian Pacific grain train, led by Union Pacific EMD SD9043MAC No. 8298, passes through Yahk, British Columbia, on 24 July 2011. In 1.3 miles at Curzon, the train will head south towards a connection to UP and the US at Kingsgate.

Canadian Pacific's wayfreight between Cranbrook and Golden begins its trip up CP's Windermere Subdivision and is approaching Wasa, British Columbia, in the Kootenay River Valley on 21 September 2013. A pair of EMD locomotives powers the northbound train – CP No. 5866 in current red and No. 5759 in CP Rail 'Action red' colours.

The southbound Canadian Pacific Golden to Cranbrook wayfreight passes a small trackside pond south of Wasa, British Columbia, on 15 July 2011. Five aging, but still classy, CP Rail EMD SD40-2s pull the train, with No. 5953 leading Nos 5727, 5993, 6011 and 6071.

On 21 September 2013, Canadian Pacific GE ES44AC No. 8710 hustles through Wasa, British Columbia, with an empty coal train heading for a crew change at Fort Steele. CP No. 8710 was built by General Electric Transportation System's sprawling 350-acre locomotive plant just outside Erie, Pennsylvania, in November 2005.

Canadian Pacific's wayfreight between Golden and Cranbrook switches the large Tembec paper plant at Skookumchuck, British Columbia, on 15 July 2011. The local is powered by EMD SD40-2 Nos 5844 and 5869, painted in CP Rail 'Action red'.

In a grand view from a hillside above Canal Flats, British Columbia, a northbound Canadian Pacific coal train rumbles over the causeway on CP's scenic Windermere Subdivision on 5 July 2014. At Canal Flats, a 1.2-mile-wide berm separates the headwaters of the Columbia from the Kootenay River. Originally called McGillivray's Portage, a canal was completed between Columbia Lake and the Kootenay in 1889, with the town's name changing to Canal Flats in 1913.

A matching pair of CP Rail 'Multimark' SD40-2s rolls the southbound Canadian Pacific wayfreight between Golden and Cranbrook through Fairmont, British Columbia, on 6 July 2014. The black and white Multimark logo and stripes used on the rear of CP Rail locomotives since 1968 was gradually phased out to a simplified scheme of red stripes both fore and aft, beginning in September 1987.

Canadian Pacific's wayfreight from Golden to Cranbrook arrives at Windermere, British Columbia, on the morning of 21 September 2002. The local will set out the grain hoppers on the rear of the train in the siding here before heading south to switch the paper mill at Skookumchuck.

Canadian Pacific's northbound wayfreight passes milepost 115 north of Harrogate, British Columbia, on 3 October 2010. The trees are quickly changing over to the colourful shades of autumn on the scenic Windermere Subdivision. It is somewhat rare by this late date to get all three EMD SD40-2s in matching CP Rail Multimark paint schemes.

On 6 July 2014, Canadian Pacific's wayfreight heads towards Golden, passing Castledale, British Columbia, through the engaging scenery along the Columbia River. Trailing leading loco EMD SD40-2 No. 6036 is a former Soo Line EMD SD60, now CP No. 6238.

Casting a reflection on the still backwaters of the Columbia River, Canadian Pacific GE ES44AC No. 8873 brings a coal empty through Harrogate, British Columbia, on the morning of 24 July 2011. CP No. 8873 was built in January 2008 and still looks pretty good in the bright morning light.

Many of the morning clouds hanging over the distant mountains haven't burned off yet on 16 July 2011 as an empty Canadian Pacific coal train led by GE AC4400CW No. 9752 heads south at McMurdo, British Columbia.

On Canadian Pacific's Thompson Subdivision between Kamloops and North Bend, British Columbia, an eastbound Canadian Pacific coal train follows the shore of Kamloops Lake at a location called Dodge, east of Savona, on 29 September 2015.

A westbound Canadian Pacific intermodal train is just east of Savona at Dodge, British Columbia, along the deep blue waters of Kamloops Lake on 6 July 2004. Powering the train are CP Rail EMD SD40-2 No. 5996 and Soo Line EMD SD60 No. 6022. CP gained full control over Soo Line Corporation in 1990, and by the time of this photograph was integrating it into its own system.

On 22 July 2011, an eastbound Canadian National freight crosses the Thompson River between Walhachin and Savona, British Columbia. This is one of seven remarkable crossings CN makes of the Thompson River while heading downstream to the confluence into the Fraser River at Lytton. Two GE products lead the train – CN No. 2261, an ES44DC built in October 2007, and CN No. 2599, a C44-9W built in January 1998.

Eastbound Canadian National intermodal train 112, led by lone EMD SD70M-2 No. 8852, crosses the Thompson River between Walhachin and Savona, British Columbia, on 22 July 2011. Note the interesting open bulkhead containers loaded with wheelsets on the train.

BC Rail GE C40-8Mu No. 4619 leads a westbound Canadian National train beginning its trek over the Thompson River east of Ashcroft, British Columbia, on 28 September 2014. CN received twenty-six of these upgraded cowl units with the acquisition of BC Rail in 2004.

Canadian National train 106 crosses over the Thompson River just east of Ashcroft, British Columbia, on a sunny 28 September 2015. Canadian Pacific's main line can be seen to the left, along with Ashcroft Terminal, which is served with a CP spur. Ashcroft Terminal is a dry port and private transloading facility, container storage and distribution centre – and at 320 acres, is British Columbia's largest inland terminal.

Canadian National train 101 departs out of the siding at Ashcroft, British Columbia, on a hot 15 July 2014. Powering the westbound service is a pair of EMD SD70M-2s, Nos 8918 and 8885, mated with blue BC Rail GE C44-9W No. 4654.

A westbound Canadian National grain train crosses the Thompson River at Ashcroft, British Columbia, on 1 September 2007. Leading the train is one of CN's comfort cab-equipped GMD SD40-2Ws, No. 5267, along with GE C44-9W No. 2627.

Canadian Pacific coal trains meet at Ashcroft, British Columbia, on the morning of 7 July 2004. Three CP AC4400CWs haul a loaded train west along the Thompson River, with the town of Ashcroft visible in the background at the end of the train.

As low sun dances off craggy cliffs on a windy, almost stormy afternoon in British Columbia, a westbound Canadian Pacific coal train makes an appearance through Black Canyon, along the Thompson River west of Ashcroft, on 24 September 2015.

Westbound Canadian National manifest freight 355 slinks through the rugged depths of Black Canyon, west of Ashcroft, British Columbia, on the afternoon of 28 September 2015. At this location in the heart of the spectacular canyon, CN's main line curves westbound through a long tunnel and immediately crosses the Thompson River on a truss bridge.

A Canadian National intermodal train curves through Black Canyon on the Thompson River near Ashcroft, British Columbia, on 25 June 2006. The train is bending through the 1,366-foot-long curved Tunnel 54.8, pulled by EMD SD75I locomotives Nos 5722 and 5758.

On the crisp morning of 25 June 2006, a westbound Canadian National intermodal train rumbles through scenic Black Canyon, west of Ashcroft, British Columbia. Powering the train are EMD SD70M-2 No. 8020 and GE C40-8M No. 2454.

A Canadian Pacific grain train swings through the curves in Black Canyon on the Thompson River west of Ashcroft, British Columbia, on 25 June 2006. A pair each of General Electric ES44AC and AC4400CW locomotives powers the westbound train, led by ES44AC No. 8744.

Canadian National GE C44-9W No. 2606 and GE C40-8M cowl No. 2430 lead a westbound freight passing through Black Canyon, west of Ashcroft, British Columbia, on the morning of 25 June 2006. In the foreground is Canadian Pacific's parallel main line and the beginning of double track to Basque, while the tunnel visible above the train is CP's Black Canyon Tunnel.

A Canadian Pacific stack train exits the Black Canyon Tunnel west of Ashcroft, British Columbia, on 25 June 2006. Two GE AC4400CWs power the train, led by No. 9707. The Canadian National line also traversing the scenic canyon can be seen closer to the Thompson River, while the former grade of the single-track CP is in between, which was abandoned when upgraded double track was extended here to the east shortly before this photograph was taken.

Two General Electric C40-8M cowl units lead a westbound Canadian National freight along the Thompson River west of Basque, British Columbia, on the afternoon of 1 September 2007. The CN and Canadian Pacific main lines from Basque to Mission, British Columbia, operate using directional running to make train operations more efficient for both railroads. CN normally sees traffic moving westbound, while eastbound trains normally use the CP.

A Canadian National freight follows the Thompson River eastbound of Spences Bridge, British Columbia, on 1 September 2007. Motive power for the freight is CN EMD SD70M-2 No. 8011 and Illinois Central EMD SD40-2 No. 6261, a former Burlington Northern locomotive now painted in CN colours.

The westbound Rocky Mountaineer Railtours passenger train hurries through Martel, east of Spences Bridge, British Columbia, on 25 September 2015, while an eastbound Canadian National intermodal train passes by on the opposite bank of the Thompson River over on Canadian Pacific's main line. The uniquely painted train is led by former CN GMD GP40-2LW No. 8011.

A westbound Canadian National intermodal train pops out of Tunnel 67.6 just east of Martel, British Columbia, in the Thompson River Canyon on the morning of 26 September 2015, led by GE ES44DC No. 2245 and EMD SD70M-2 No. 8839.

A westbound Canadian Pacific coal train curves along the Thompson River at Martel, British Columbia, on 6 July 2004. Lone GE AC4400CW No. 9781 leads the train, assisted by another AC4400CW linked as a rear DPU.

Curving along the Thompson River is a westbound Canadian National intermodal train between Martel and Spences Bridge, British Columbia, on 28 September 2001. Powering the train is GMD SD50F No. 5436, leading GMD SD40-2W Nos 5352 and 5288.

On the afternoon of 22 July 2011, a westbound Canadian Pacific freight powered by GE AC4400CW Nos 9739 and 9641 curves along the cool waters of the Thompson River between Martel and Spences Bridge, British Columbia.

A Canadian Pacific coal train powered by a trio of GE AC4400CW locomotives – Nos 9589, 9682 and 8509 – is west of Spences Bridge, British Columbia, on 7 July 2004. Somewhat unusually, this train is westbound on the CP main line, which is normally reserved for eastbound traffic on this section of directional running with Canadian National between Mission (east of Vancouver) and Basque (west of Ashcroft).

Softly reflecting in the Thompson River, a westbound Canadian Pacific potash train passes through the Skoonka Tunnels west of Spences Bridge, British Columbia, on a sunny 27 September 2015. The unit train of Canpotex cars is led by GE ES44AC Nos 9353 and 8888.

Trains meet in the Thompson River Canyon as a westbound Canadian Pacific coal train approaches Seddall west of Spences Bridge, British Columbia, on Canadian National trackage, while on the other side of the river at Drynoch, an eastbound CN intermodal train is using the CP main line on 27 September 2001.

An eastbound Canadian National freight hustles eastbound along the Thompson River at Drynoch, British Columbia, on 28 September 2001. Powering the train is a pair of former CN GMD SD40s now owned by Alstom, but still lettered GEC Alsthom Transport, and rebuilt into SD40-3s.

Canadian National manifest freight 301 is westbound in a scenic setting along the Thompson River between Seddall and Morris, British Columbia, on 26 September 2015. Motive power for 301 this particular morning is provided by EMD SD70M-2 No. 8849 and GE C44-9W No. 2534.

Traveling westbound through Thompson River Canyon, west of Drynoch, British Columbia, on 5 July 2004 is a Canadian National passenger train. The train is on Canadian Pacific rails, and is piloted by newly minted CP AC4400CW No. 9807, with brightly painted CN E9A Nos 102 and 103 trailing the big GE on a five-car train.

On 16 July 2014, an eastbound Canadian Pacific track geometry train is west of Drynoch, British Columbia, inspecting the CP main line. The diminutive train is pulled by GP20C-ECO No. 2241, one of 130 units rebuilt between 2012 and 2015 from GP7u and GP9u locomotives, utilising components such as trucks, traction motors, main generators and air compressors from these donor units.

Canadian National stack trains pass each other on opposite sides of the Thompson River on 1 September 2007. The eastbound train led by EMD SD60F No. 5525 is on Canadian Pacific rails west of Drynoch on this shared directional running section of the railroad, while on the other side of the Thompson, the CN train is between Seddall and Morris on its home railroad.

Along a low, but still turbulent Thompson River is a westbound Canadian National freight east of Morris, British Columbia, on 27 September 2001. Locomotives on the train are a pair of GMD SD50F Nos 5443 and 5409, along with rebuilt GMD SD40u No. 6024. CN No. 6024 was built in 1968 and remanufactured in 1995 with Dash 2 specifications, extended dynamic brakes and with the installation of a Q-Tron microprocessor, leading to it being labelled by some as a SD40-2Q.

Negotiating at least six curves at once, a Canadian Pacific stack train led by GE ES44AC No. 8789 and GE AC4400CW No. 8619 heads west at Morris, British Columbia, on Canadian National's Ashcroft Subdivision in the Thompson River Canyon on 24 September 2012.

An eastbound Canadian Pacific empty coal train passes below Skihist Provincial Park on 25 September 2015. On the other side of the Thompson River, a Canadian National work train continues loading fallen rock into Difco dump cars in CN's never-ending battle with nature along this rugged and unforgiving piece of main line between Morris and Lasha, east of Lytton, British Columbia.

Battling the ongoing effort to keep the Canadian National route through White Canyon open is a work train powered by CN SD75I No. 5731, seen passing through multiple rockslide sheds between Morris and Lasha, British Columbia, on 27 September 2015. This scenic canyon along the Thompson River requires constant attention from what nature dishes out, and this train will soon be loading more fallen rock into its eleven Difco dump cars for removal to Spences Bridge.

Canadian National SD70M-2 No. 8862 and GE C44-9W No. 2553, along with lone rear DPU SD70M-2 No. 8000, power a westbound Canpotex potash train in White Canyon between Morris and Lasha, British Columbia, on 27 September 2015.

On 27 September 2015, an eastbound Canadian Pacific empty coal train led by GE ES44AC No. 8709 passes milepost 92 on CP tracks east of Lytton, British Columbia, in the Thompson River Canyon. In the background are the rugged walls of White Canyon.

A unit train of tank cars on a westbound Canadian Pacific train crosses the Thompson River on Canadian National's Ashcroft Subdivision at Lytton, British Columbia, on 7 July 2004. A trio of CP GE AC4400CWs provides locomotion for the westbound train – Nos 9602, 9816 and 9665.

A westbound Canadian National freight crosses the Fraser River over Cisco Bridge at Cisco, British Columbia, on 27 September 2001. Powering the train is the interesting consist of EMD SD50F No. 5450 leading a trio of former CN SD40s now owned by Alstom, but still lettered GEC Alsthom Transport, and rebuilt into SD40-3s. CN's Cisco Bridge is 247 meters (810 feet) long and 67 meters (220 feet) high, and also crosses over the parallel Canadian Pacific main line.

Snaking through serpentine trackage in British Columbia's Fraser River Canyon is a westbound Canadian Pacific freight train at Conrad on 28 September 2001. A pair of GE AC4400CWs powers the train – CP No. 8635 and blue CEFX No. 1004.

The westbound Rocky Mountaineer Railtours passenger train approaches Boston Bar, British Columbia, along the Fraser River on 28 September 2001. The train is painted in its former livery of dark blue and white with red striping, and is curving past the old main line bridge over Stoyoma Creek on Canadian National.

Westbound Canadian Pacific and Canadian National trains sit in Boston Bar, British Columbia, on 28 September 2001. The CP intermodal train is led by GE AC4400CW No. 8569, while the CN coal train has distinctive EMD SD60F No. 5523 in the lead.

A westbound Canadian National freight leaves Boston Bar, British Columbia, and crosses the Anderson River Bridge on 27 September 2001. The train is led by GMD SD60F No. 5540 and GMD SD40-2W No. 5266, and has a good cut of Procor tank cars up front.

Curving across Anderson River Bridge, 2 miles from Boston Bar, British Columbia, is a Canadian Pacific freight heading west through the Fraser Canyon on 28 September 2001. Yes, one of the crew is taking a photograph of us photographing the train!

A westbound Canadian National intermodal train exits a tunnel and immediately crosses Ainslie Creek over a high bridge in this rugged portion of the canyon near Martinson, British Columbia, on 28 September 2001. Powering the train is an all-GMD consist of SD50F No. 5436 leading SD40-2W Nos 5352 and 5288.

Led by Canadian National GE C44-9W No. 2681, an eastbound CN grain train blasts out of the Yale Tunnel at Yale, British Columbia, in the craggy Fraser River Canyon on 24 September 2012. The nearby town of Yale, established in 1848, was reportedly in its heyday the largest 'city' west of Chicago and north of San Francisco.

An eastbound Canadian Pacific grain train powered by GE ES44AC No. 8949, along with an older AC4400CW, crosses the Spuzzum Creek Bridge at Spuzzum, British Columbia, on 24 September 2012, in a trip through the awesome Fraser River Canyon.

Far below the towering cliffs surrounding Fraser River Canyon at Yale, British Columbia, is a westbound Canadian Pacific train heading for Vancouver on 8 July 2004. A pair of colourful GE AC4400CWs provides power for the train – a red CP No. 8635 and a leased blue CEFX No. 1004.

Canadian Pacific EMD SD40-2F No. 9006 leads an eastbound train at East Mission, British Columbia, on 26 September 2001. These custom-built cowled machines were built exclusively for CP more than two years after the last SD40-2s were outshopped by EMD. Built by GMD in London, Ontario, in November 1988, these twenty-five units were numbered 9000–9024 and later earned the nickname 'Red Barns.'

A pair of Canadian Pacific GE AC4400CWs tugs an eastbound stack train past CP caboose No. 434556 tucked in a siding at Mission, British Columbia, on 31 August 2007. In Canada, cabooses were frequently known as 'vans' on both CP and CN.

Three Southern Railway of British Columbia locomotives sit by the SRY yard office at Vye Road in Huntingdon, British Columbia, on 23 June 2006. SRY MP15DC No. 152 and SW900 Nos 906 and 907 are all former British Columbia Hydro. This railroad is owned by parent company in the United States, the Washington Companies, which also owns Montana Rail Link.

A pair of switcher locomotives rests at Canadian National's yard at North Vancouver, British Columbia, on 2 September 2007. On the left is CN GMD SW1200RM No. 7304 mated to GMD GMD-1u No. 1419 (not visible), and on the right is GMD GMD-1u No. 1408 mated to SW1200RM No. 7311. General Motors Diesel built 101 GMD-1 1,200 hp switchers between August 1958 and April 1960, with five going to Northern Alberta Railways (NAR) and the rest being built for CN.

Canadian National GMD-1u No. 1421, along with GP9RM (GP9u) No. 7055, switches the grain elevators along Low Level Road at North Vancouver, British Columbia, on 26 September 2001. Four Canadian geese walk alongside the train, seemingly asking for some of the train's contents.

BC Rail (formerly British Columbia Railway, and before that Pacific Great Eastern) General Electric C40-8Mu Nos 4622 and 4601 bracket the West Coast Railway Association's Canadian Pacific GMD FP7 No. 4069 in the BCR locomotive facility at North Vancouver, British Columbia, on 26 September 2001.

BC Rail GE C40-8Mu locomotives gather at the railroad's engine facility at North Vancouver, British Columbia, on a rainy 26 September 2001. BCR had twenty-six of these cowled GEs, which were upgraded from 4,000 hp to 4,400 hp and Dash 9 standards by the railroad. All twenty-six went to Canadian National when that railroad acquired BCR in July 2004.

VIA Rail's eastbound Canadian departs Vancouver, British Columbia, and is only minutes into its journey out of Pacific Central Station at CN Junction on 2 September 2007. Three EMD F40PH-2 locomotives power the train under the curving bridge of Vancouver's Expo Skytrain.